Secrets
Of
The Holy City
Mecca

Volume One

By Rasheed L. Muhammad

Table of Content

Acknowledgment

This acknowledgement is written to thank many that have influenced my journey. I thank Bro. Harvey J. X Robinson of Muhammad Mosque #8, Bro. Stanley Muhammad of Muhammad Mosque #27, Bro. Jabril Muhammad of Muhammad Mosque #32, Bro. Halim Muhammad of Mosque #27, Bro. Shahid Muhammad of Mosque #27, *Dr. A. K. Muhammad*, Bro. Victor Muhammad of Muhammad Mosque #11, Bro. Wendell Muhammad of Mosque #27, Mother Tynetta Muhammad, wife of the Honorable Elijah Muhammad, Bro. Rasul Muhammad of the seventh Region, *Capt.* Malik Muhammad of Muhammad Mosque #27, Bro. Marvin Muhammad of Muhammad Mosque #54, Jim Brown, Football Haller Famer. Thanks to my brother D. Rasheed, my sister Sandra, my mother and father, Sister Erica Muhammad of Muhammad Mosque #28, Coach D., and Bro. Alfonso X of Muhammad Mosque #8. Lastly, I thank Allah for not discarding the role and purpose of the Asiatic Black Nation whom this world has all but written out of white history. Of what He has blessed me to write since 1986 on many subjects has taken 24 years to get out into a 14-book presentation. These books are only more evidence to demonstrate that Black America have indeed received two Divine servants of Allah, i.e., Elijah Muhammad and Minister Farrakhan and God (Allah) has not forsaken His people no matter how bleak our circumstances under the current global leadership.

Other books by the Author:

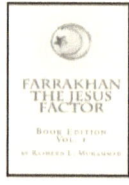

All Books are available contact noidecoded@yahoo.com

The term Arabia comes from Old-Persian where it is pronounced 'Arab'ya'. One value Arabs held high was maintaining the purity of the Holy Quran. They also took pride in maintaining historical events and lineage, especially with respect to the Prophet of Islam, Mohammed Ibn Abdullah.

This book evinces how the history of Mohammed's tribe contained some of the secret prophetic history of Black America, Elijah Muhammad and the Founder of the Nation of Islam in the Western Hemisphere, Master Wallace Fard Muhammad who was also born in Mecca, Arabia.

For the most part, the Nation of Islam demonstrates how Jewish and Christian biblical scriptures pointed toward Black America's 400-year sojourn in America by using the principles of historical and theological congruency. However, the history of Mecca, Arabia and some of its profound families will now be employed to also demonstrate how their history is also mathematically and theologically congruent with respect to Black America's sojourn in America from slavery to Islam.

Although Black people's divine history is more pronounced in the Bible than in the Quran, it is yet hidden there in a secret codified letter system under the name Al-Muquatta'at.

The Arabic word Al-Muqatta'at—derived from the root 'qata'a' - to cut, and means 'what is cut' and also 'what is abbreviated'. Hence, the Quran abbreviated or "cuts out" what would happen to a certain tribe of people from Africa during the last days that serve as slaves in a strange land. On the other hand, if reiterate, the bible records it in more detail, but in a conundrum based upon Caucasian Jewish and Gentile religious scholarship mixed with truth and falsehood.

Had the original ancient divine writers of history included those parts of divine history regarding Prophets Mohammed predecessors (family members) as they did with the predecessors of Abraham, Moses, David, Solomon etc, it would have made it too easy for the enemy to figure out exactly how and where the crusher of the wicked (Christ) would be born.

Al-Suyooty's ITQAAN, First Printing, 1318 AH, Vol 2, on page 10 of his book wrote, "Jews in Medina questioned Prophet Mohammed about muqatta'at. They went to the Prophet and said, "Your Quran is initialed with A.L.M., and these Initials determine the life span of your religion. Since `A' is 1, `L' is 30, and `M' is 40, this means that your religion will survive only 71 years." Muhammad said, "We also have A.L.M.S." They said, "The `A' is 1, the `L' is 30, the `M' is 40, and the `S' is 90. This adds up to 161. Do you have anything else?" The Prophet said, "Yes, A.L.M.R." They said, "This is longer and heavier; the `A' is 1, `L' is 30, `M' is 40, and `R' is 200, making the total 271." They finally gave up, saying, 'We do not know how many of these Initials he was given!' "

As it were, the muqatta'at letters were designed to hide the history of the life and times of Messenger Elijah Muhammad, Minister Farrakhan and an enslaved people; in the *mysterious* New World. That new world was North America where Africans served physical servitude under several

European governments (including Britain, Spain and America) from year [1555] or 1619 to 1776. Then when Blacks finally gained civil rights through the Supreme Court system of the U.S. in 1965, they legally gained status as American citizens, which was approximately 400 years after arriving in the New World.[1]

Today with the revelation and manifestation of Minister Louis Farrakhan Muhammad (whose wisdom flows like the Well of Zam Zam in Mecca, Arabia), all former divine histories are drawing to a halt, thus opening a way for something entirely new.

All Mighty God Allah desires to make America's formers slaves the head and not the tail. He intends to put the exslave in heaven foremost.

Rasheed L. Muhammad
September 19, 2010
Sunday 9:55 pm

---

[1] Chapter 10 Quran Verse, By Rasheed L. Muhammad

Chapter 1

Slavery In Mecca, Arabia

During the days of ignorance, around 1,500 years ago Mecca Arabia practiced slavery. One of its most famous slaves was Bilal. According to history, this child was a descendant of a people who were kidnapped from Africa and sold on the Mecca slave market. Subsequently, he never discovered who his real fore parents and brothers and sisters were in Africa when he became a grown man. What he knew of Africa and other places came through stories he had heard other slaves tell. Bilal soon learned to speak his slave masters language—the Arabic language. He also worked hard loading merchandise on camels and ran many errands for his slave master—a rich man about Mecca.

Bilal's history was used by God (Allah) and the writers of divine scripture (history) to hide the future predicament of African people during the Atlantic slave trade, which began as early has 1555 AD. This is the time when

Africans of the old world brought to North America were being bred to physically and mentally serve Caucasian slave masters in the new world. As events got worse, so did the rules governing Black slaves.

To the same degree, the rules governing all slaves (both male and female) in Mecca stipulated (1) no slave could journey outside of Mecca without his masters permission, (2) no slave could marry without his masters permission, (3) a slave could not own money without his master permission, and (4) if a slave was beaten by his master, the slave could not accuse the master in a court of justice. If this sounds similar to the conditions set upon U.S. slaves, take it for what its worth. History does repeat itself.

Bilal Hears About Mohammed

Many slaves in Mecca would meet during the night speaking with one another about their experiences or what they had overheard their masters say. Some even told stories about their journey to Mecca from their own country.

12

But one night a slave began to talk about a man named Mohammed, an honest merchant with true sincerity and generosity. In addition to mentioning the outstanding characteristics about this man Mohammed, the word among the slaves was that Mohammed said: "there was only One God and this One God commands people be just." However, before that night ended, another slave was recorded to have said, "it makes no difference because the rich men of Mecca are not going to listen anyway...they always want to keep everything to themselves...every opportunity to rule..."

Naturally, the new message of Mohammed 1,400 years ago in which Bilal and the other slaves were hearing was publicly ridiculed by the rich and well-to-do people of Mecca.

Jewish scripture speaks about a rich man and a captive named Lazarus {Luke 16:19-21}. It reads, *19 "There was a rich man who was dressed in purple and fine linen and lived in luxury every day. 20 At his gate was laid a beggar named Lazarus, covered with sores 21 and longing to eat what*

13

fell from the rich man's table. Even the dogs came and licked his sores." Here again, God (Allah) and the writers of divine scripture hide the history of white America and black America—the former slaves under the name Lazarus. So rather than the rich man representing certain Meccans, he (they) in the last days represented Europe's Jewish and Gentile merchant class of rich exploiters of the initial Black slaves abused and misused in the new world now famously known as America.

Slaves Accept Islam

All slaves began hearing about Mohammed, though not yet as Allah's seal of the prophets. He became acceptable to the slaves of Mecca because he always sided with the poor and oppressed people. After three years of preaching in the city of Mecca, Mohammed publicly declared himself as the Messenger of Allah. When his following grew in number, he became a stronger force for the rich to reckon.

Zaid, one of Bilal's acquaintances, was a free man. He was also known as the son of Mohammed. One day Zaid invited

Bilal to meet with Prophet Mohammed. When *Bilal al-Habashi* initially arrived at Mohammed's house, there were a number of males and females, boys and girls. At the end of the meeting, the Prophet closed in prayer. From that day forward, Bilal went to the Prophets house whenever he could get away from his slave masters job. On one occasion, his slave master had heard that he was attending with Mohammed and demanded Bilal go no more. When Bilal refused, he was beaten. In fact, his rich slave master attempted to torture him even to the point of death while demanding he keep believing in the old gods of Mecca and forsake Mohammed and Allah. To those aware, this image of what happened to Bilal in Mecca, Arabia practically describes what happened to Kunta Kinta in Alex Hailey's movie Roots. Recall the scene how his slave master beat him nearly to death until Kunta Kinta finally accepted the slave masters name Toby, but not his religion...

The question becomes, how many young men and women of today have been tormented by their employers, friends and/or parents for attempting to accept Islam as they sought a better life than the one they had practiced under the old religion of this modern world?

Mohammed Frees The African Slave Bilal

After the news of atrocities committed upon Bilal reached Prophet Muhammad (PBUH), he sent his most trusted companion Abu Bakr to buy Bilal's freedom.[2] The tortured body of Bilal was seen by many but his life was speared from the cruel hand of his evil slave master.

While recovering at the home of Abu Bakr, he told Bilal "Allah's messenger(s) does not want human beings to be slaves. He wants them to be free servants of Allah." The good acts of Abu Bakr were carried out in accordance with what the Prophet of Islam had asked him to do. Furthermore, this good act reminds one about the Parable of the Good Samaritan mentioned in Luke 10: 33-33, *"But a Samaritan, as he traveled, came where the man was; and when he saw him, he took pity on him. [34] He went to him and bandaged his wounds, pouring on oil and wine. Then he put the man on his*

---

[2] http://www.helium.com/items/1516807-bilal-prophet-mazen-adhan-azan-habshi

own donkey, took him to an inn and took care of him." As you may see, the Biblical parable was a real event that also took place in the Holy City Mecca between Bilal and Abu Bakr by the request of Prophet Mohammed (Peace Be Upon Him).

So here again, God (Allah) and the writers of divine scripture hide the history of Black America—U.S. former slaves—under a biblical parable and an event that had occurred in Mecca, Arabia.

However, in the fullness of time, the relationship between the Good Samaritan and the wounded man represents the coming of God in Person who finds His people among enemies. Subsequently, a process was initiated to heal their wounds over time. Black America and the Nation of Islam in North America are still living under that time now for they are the antitype of all previous types who rehearsed the Good Samaritan and wounded man enactment from Jerusalem to Arabia.

The truth that will set any slave free is Islam and its entire scope, science and legislative essence for humans and a society for humans. Jesus said, *"And ye shall know the truth and the truth shall make you free." (John 8:32)*

Bilal Type Antitype of Black Slaves in America

Over the years, Bilal became the Prophets official muezzin (caller to prayer). He was chosen to call all of the early Muslims to pray. Moreover, Bilal being chosen to call the righteous to prayer represented a sign and future assignment of Black men and women of America where the ultimate fulfillment will only manifest after their 400-year sojourn in North America absolutely terminates.

Prophet Muhammad (PBUH) once said of Bilal's future: "he heard the resonance of Bilal's footsteps ahead of him in the heavens...."[3]

During these end times or since the founding of the new world in North America, Black peoples true divine role and purpose was once hidden secretly beneath prophesy and other cryptic sayings, which pointed toward a people that

---

[3] http://www.helium.com/items/1516807-bilal-prophet-mazen-adhan-azan-habshi

18

would also rule heaven on earth when such time is made manifest. Over the past five to six hundred years, the nations of the earth have been ruled by members of the white race. Most original people generally refer to this race as the devil because to the hell they have scientifically raised around our globe, in the seas, mountains, atmosphere and deserts. You name it, the white race have destroyed it since leaving Europe in 1492.

Former Slaves To Establish Heaven On Earth

In terms of a heavenly existence being established on earth, Jesus said, *"let Thy kingdom come; let Thy will be done, as in Heaven so on earth;"* (Bible Matthew 6:10)

1973 Saviours Day, the Honorable Elijah Muhammad taught:

"We are the people to look forward to the....toward the making of heaven and earth, as we are going to do it. At least...I'm not saying I'm going to do it, but I'm helping now. This is why that you repeatedly hear something from the first. How it was done.

"If you have caught up with the wisdom of that first man, then it needs a second man to change the whole thing around because you are not supposed to be standing aimless...No. After the first God, we are practically, now, peeping into some of His artwork.

19

And finding in the root of this art work a way to change up the whole thing. This is why, again, that it is promised to you and me -- a new heaven and a new earth. Some of us say that is spiritually. Yes it is, at the present."

Neither European Gentile or Jewish style capitalism nor Mecca's old civilization will rule the order of the day like Allah intends to establish through the ex-slaves. Nevertheless, old world civilizations and their ancient biblical characters, significant figures, families and a choice of divine life events were rehearsed as the Quran and Bible indicate.

The Bible says,

*"Symeon hath **rehearsed** how first God visited the Gentiles, to take out of them a people for his name." (Acts 15:14)*

The Holy Quran says,

*[6] But there are, among men, those who purchase idle tales, without knowledge (or meaning), to mislead (men) from the Path of Allah and throw ridicule (on the Path): for such there will be a Humiliating Penalty. [7] When Our Signs are **rehearsed** to such a one, he turns away in arrogance, as if he heard them not, as if there were deafness in both his ears: announce to him a grievous Penalty." (Holy Quran 31:6-7)*

Many types were rehearsed, carried out and are now being finalized by America's former slaves during these last days of the coming of God in Person and the fall of America—the rule of the white race.

It Is Written

Although there may be those who might say "slavery" happened a long time ago, a long time ago in the eyes and Judgment of God is no time at all.

The good book says 1,000 years to man is merely a day to God {Holy Quran 32:5} *"He arranges [each] matter from the heaven to the earth; then it will ascend to Him in a Day, the extent of which is a 1,000 years of those which you count."* This is why it takes 25,000 years for the history of man to complete one cycle according to God's clock. He uses the precession of earth's motion and the actions of earth's original people to complete the days of judgement under a scientific process called precession.

Precession is a change in the orientation of the rotation axis of a rotating body. As the earth rotates, her

polar axis point toward the heavens (stars) at an incline of 23.3 degrees and she axis slowly traces out a cone. Under this presure, the Earth [wobbles from the sun and moon pulling upon her liquids] goes through one such complete precessional cycle in a period of approximately 26,000 [and/or 25,000] years, during which the positions of stars as measured in the equatorial coordinate system will slowly change; the change is actually due to the change of the coordinates. Over this cycle the Earth's north axial pole moves from where it is now, within 1 degree of Polaris, in a circle around the ecliptic pole, with an angular radius of about 23.5 degrees. The shift is 1 degree in 72 years, where the angle is taken from the observer, not from the center of the circle.[4] Although the earth is spinning around the sun at 1,037.3 milers per hour, we don't physically feel its G-Forces nor her wobble because of Allah's Law. What we feel is a spiritual wobble wherein from time to time we stubble and fall because everyone is pulling on everything for its stability, including the sun, moon and stars. And, between wife and husband, a child pulls upon them consequently, we wobble. Thus man needs Divine guidance and Divine History.

In a word or two, divine history is derived from above because it was first written in celestial splendor, light years before man received its text or messages. The earth is like a compass used that points toward the heavenly stars above wherein prehistory is transmitted, recorded and revealed through divine prophets and also carried out through significant events of many individuals or certain tribes. From this source came much spiritual guidance and scripture.

"We will note that as we travel the globe all original societies and people trace their origin to the star system and from there they trace their origins back to the earth. Physically, mentally and

---

[4] http://en.wikipedia.org/wiki/Precession

spiritually, we are connected in our origin to stardust, which contains the genetic material of our DNA that is transmitted from our Milky Way Galaxy to the human species of man. Thus, the Honorable Elijah Muhammad teaches us that our history is written in the stars and that our ancient forefathers (scientists) simply willed a star or stars into being, and within a few thousand, million or trillions of years down the line of time, those thoughts brought our world into existence.

In the preface of his book, "Message to the Blackman in America," he (HEM) states: "As we near the exhaustion of the Wisdom of this world which has not been able to shed enough light on our path in search for that Supreme Wisdom to keep us from stumbling and falling, we now seek the wisdom of Allah, the Best Knower and Guide in the Person of Master Fard Muhammad (to Whom be praised forever). The reader will find that light in this book." [5]

[5] www.finalcall.com/artman/publish/article_6100.shtml

Chapter II

God Hidden in Black Arab Lineage

In the Islamic world, the birth of the Holy One for which a body was prepared as the Divine Supreme Being (Allah) or Al-Mahdi. The Christians refer to this Holy One as Christ meaning crusher of evil.

"Wherefore, coming into the world, he saith, 'Sacrifice and offering Thou didst not will, and a body Thou didst prepare for me..." *(Hebrews 10:5)*

A part of the history about Him whose body was especially prepared was also hidden in the history of Prophet Mohammed's family—a Black Arab lineage. As a consequence, one of the secrets of the Holy City Mecca.

Traditionalists propound Mohammed's lineage directly ties him to Prophet Abraham through Prophet Ishmael down to the man Adnan, to Qusay, to Hashim. After reading through the family events and its major characters, you'll discover how some of Arabia's Black tribes, placed after all others, ultimately produced the Great Mahdi of the Muslims and

25

Messiah of the Christians in the Personage of Master W. Fard Muhammad. This Holy One, Israel was forewarned would come by the writings of Prophet Moses {Genesis 15:12-13} *[12]As the sun was about to set, a trance fell upon Abram, and a deep, terrifying darkness enveloped him. [13] Then the LORD said to Abram: 'Know for certain that your descendants shall be aliens (strangers) in a land not their own, where they shall be enslaved and oppressed for four hundred years. [14] But I will bring judgment on the nation they must serve, and in the end they will depart with great wealth."*

Recall from the Bible how Ishmael was Abraham's first-born son produced by Hagar, a Black women whom he took into the Desert of Arabia with her son. When Abraham left them, Ishmael and Hagar were practically not even mentioned by western Christian people, let alone ancient Black people whom Hagar and Ishmael represented.

At least the Jewish Encyclopedia provides some rehearsed historical insight about these two significant Black people mentioned in divine history.

"Egyptian handmaid [Hagar] of Sarah, and mother of Ishmael. According to one narrative, Sarah, having no children, requested Abraham to take Hagar as concubine, so that she might adopt her children (comp. "Gen. xxx. 3, where Rachel makes a similar request). When Hagar had conceived she became domineering, and Sarah, with the consent of Abraham, drove her into the wilderness. There, as she sat by a fountain, an angel of the Lord appeared and commanded her to return to her mistress and submit to her. He promised that she should bear a son who would be called "Ishmael" ("he whom the Lord will hear"), and that he would be a strong fighter ("a wild ass among men"), and would be respected by his brethren (Gen. xvi.).

"Another narrative tells that when Isaac had been weaned Ishmael "played" with him or "mocked" him (מצחק is ambiguous), and that Sarah demanded of Abraham that he cast out Hagar and her son, that the latter might not inherit with Isaac. Abraham was unwilling to do so, but upon God's command he yielded. Hagar fled again into the wilderness, where Ishmael came near dying of thirst. In the moment of her greatest despair an angel of God appeared to her and showed her a well, promising her that Ishmael would found a great nation. She dwelt with her son in the wilderness of Paran, where he became an archer, and she took a wife for him from Egypt." (Gen. xxi. 9-21).[6]

From Ishmael To Qusay In 1,374 Years

Ishmael lived between 1910 BC to 1774 BC. Then in 400 BC (or 1,374 years from Ishmael), Qusay was born into one of the early Black Arabian families of Koryesh (Quarish). His

---

[6] www.jewishencyclopedia.com/view.jsp?artid=53&letter=h

character is of substantial notoriety because he is the great, great, great, great grandfather of Prophet Mohammed.

According to historian Runoko Rashidi, author of "African Presence in Early Asia" he wrote that due to Qusay's prior lineage, the Black Koryesh became the ancestral guardians of the Sacred Black Stone of the Kaaba. His people were the most powerful tribe in their valley homeland that included Mecca...He persuaded Quarish to build houses around the Kaaba...Undoubtedly, it was the Black Arabian families that lived close to the Kaaba and the Red Semites who were ostracized. This seems to be the cause of the separation with the Koryesh, which caused great resentment and malignity between the Black Koryesh and the Semites (white skinned Arabs), who would later become the powerful Umayyad or Ummeyyah...Qusai is both the common ancestor of the final Muslim Prophet, Mohammed Ibn Abdullah and the Umayyad family.

Qusay won great honor and fame for his tribe, Quraish, by his wisdom. He also built the 'town hall' of Makkah, the first one in Arabia. The leaders of the various clans gathered in this hall to ponder upon their social, commercial, cultural and political problems. He formulated laws for the supply of food and water to the pilgrims who came to Makkah, and he persuaded the Arabs to pay a tax for their support.

Qusay ultimately obtained supreme power at Mecca. After he died, his son Abd Manaf, took charge of his duties. He too distinguished himself by his ability. He was noted for his generosity and good judgment. He was [finally] succeeded by his son Hashim who later father a son named Sheba.

Sheba Is Found

Hashim was the father of Sheba (also spelled Shaiba). After Hashim died, his elder brother had to retrieve and restore Sheba into authority over his fathers house, wealth and property upon his return to the Holy City Mecca. The secret history of the Holy City Mecca demonstrates that Prophet Mohammed was an offspring of Sheba. The uncle who brought him back to Mecca was named Al Muttalib. This man was Mecca's greatest entertainer at some point in time. He manifested so splendid a style as to deserve the epithet *Al Faidh*, 'the Munificent.' You might say he was a 'Charmer'. But what else should one expect, he carried the DNA of his tribe! Likewise, who are the worlds greatest entertainers today? Think this over!

In terms of an overall Type Antitype, ancient Mecca's history entails the mission of God in Person who seeks to save and to restore His fathers lost pedigree (Black man and women of America), back among the righteous people of the earth. Such history was kept from the brain trust of America's former slaves 1555 to 1934. I say around 1934 because by that year, Master Fard Muhammad had converted 25,000 Black people to the religion Islam [Nation of Islam] since His coming to America in 1930. One aspect of His teaching was that Black people; particularly, found on the continent of Africa and brought to the Americas are the lost members of the tribe of Shabazz. More details will be provided about this tribe later.

Unfortunately, the version of God coming to save a lost people from their slave masters has been a European Jewish and Christian interpretation. Consequently, most Black Americans have remained spiritually dead, deaf, dumb and blind due to fear of accepting Divine Truth and simple truth too. Yet, their mind produces twenty-four billion thoughts per second.

The Jewish Women

A further review into Hashim's history will evince, in part, from where Allah and the writers of divine history did employ the types; namely, Jewish and Arab historical events to complete the final antitypes.[7]

Let us see! Hisham fathered a child named Sheba during Arabia's pre-Islamic era. This was SALMA, a pious women, and daughter of Amr, a Khazrajite of the Bani Najjar, one of the Jewish tribes of Arabia.[8] Could this be why

---

[7] Type Antitype is for a community of people who want to offer their knowledge concerning the sanctuary service and the types of the Old Testament [old world] and how they represent things in the New Testament [new world].

[8] http://answering-islam.org/Books/Muir/Life1/chapter4.htm

Christian scriptural scientists debate how or why (of) the seven Mary's mentioned in the bible, one had seven devils removed from her soul? Could part of this history be why it has been reputed by the Nation of Islam that the mother of Master W. Fard Muhammad was a Caucasian Jewish women whom His father, Alfonso (**Arabic:** بنـــو إذفـــونش, **Banu Idfunš or Tribe of Alfonso),** was a solid black man that cleaned up a white women thus making her a Muslim before allowing her to conceive the Holy One that was going to be specially prepared {Hebrew 10:5)?

The truth of the matter is locked into the true history presented by the Nation of Islam in the west. Both Arab and Jewish lineage, their divine historical events and bright political or prophetic characters merely rehearsed future events. These events were signs of the lost members, the lost sheep, the lost coin {Luke 15:1-10} who were ultimately found in the bounds of North America by God in Personage of Master W. Fard Muhammad

The father of W. Fard Muhammad was an Islamic Scientists. The Honorable Elijah Muhammad taught regarding this subject:

"We have been lost so long...so long that it has taken one that loved us. It has taken one that was made for us out of the two people to come and seek to find us and after finding us he had to have the power to save and deliver us.

"This man had to be prepared. He was not already made and formed. He had to be prepared a form to get among us. He could not come as He was, in the spiritual form of the Nation's mind.

"So His father had to prepare this man to come find us and then take us from our captors. We have to be taken. This is why that He, Himself, had to come. *"Even I.."*, says the prophet, *"...I will go after them. I will search the earth until I find them."* A great lover with all power and with the eye to search the earth to locate that lost one.

"We are a very beloved people, for God, Himself, to come an search the Earth and the Nations to find we that was lost.... That shows how important you are, that God will not allow one of us to be lost.

"We are going to get over to you the History of This Man, Who is The Almighty God in Person, as He gave it to me. He says to me, beginning His History -- that I want you to listen carefully to -- that His father was a Black man, very much so. And His mother was a white woman.

"He said that His father knew he could not be successful in coming to a solid white country, and he being a solid Black man. So, He says to me, or rather He taught me, that His father said, "I will go and make me a son. And I will send my son among them, looking like

33

them." Think over that! "And my son, they will think he is one of them. And He will find our lost people."

"So Almighty God, in the Person of Master Fard Muhammad, says to me that he said, "I will have to make one look like them." So, He said, His father went up into the hills and there he found him a wife. A white wife. And he taken her and made a good Muslim out of her. I don't know about that fancy that we have in the Bible that he cast seven devils out of the woman to make her fit for giving birth to This Man, The Saviour. Now, I am not going to argue with no Theologian about it, because there is something in it to prepare a woman, that by nature, is born of the devil, to give birth to a Man destined to be the Ruler and God in Person, of the heavens and earth. Naturally, he had to be careful in preparing his wife.

"So He says to me, or He taught me, that He was taken by His father, after He was born, and went looking for every good book or books that contained great words of wisdom spoken by great Kings and of all great people. He said He would get a word or two for this one and a word or two from that one which was put away as a secret and he'd bring it and give it to Him. He paid the people high prices for such a word or two on the History of such-and-such man. So these things He was in preparation for a time.

"Let's go back to the hills now. He says that after finding a wife for him in the hills. I am not going into that with you right now about where the hills were at and who was called the hill. I won't go into that with you right now. Some day you will hear me tell you but I want to be sure when I tell you this that the hills will welcome me to tell you.

"We have from Him, He says to me, that His father married this woman and that the first child she birthed for him was a girl. And He said his father said, "Uhm, I missed that time!" So, He said, he made another try and that was Him. And, He said, he taken so carefully care of Him that He may be sent among the western

34

people -- the Caucasian people. Of course, their real name you have known. Of course, Caucasian is their name too. But their real name is the devil. But he needed one of these devil people in order to make complete...This is not a mockery for me to stand here and call these people the devil because that's what they are. If any mockery should be done it should be done for us. If what we have made or created then the God of Blackman should be responsible for the mockery. I want to give you the truth. They didn't make themselves. We made them! Well then, you have no right to be saying that your product is no good. Well if you made it no good then don't blame that which you made for being no good, because you made it. I know I'm coming to you in a way that you didn't think about. We are here to tell the truth.

"He's [Master Fard Muhammad] made partly from the race of Yacub and partly from His own [Black nation], just for the purpose to save you and me."[9]

In retrospect, the father of Master W. Fard Muhammad fulfilled what Hisham had rehearsed before him. Hisham's history was merely a rehearsal of something greater to come. Reviewing it with even more clarity according to authentic Arab history, it reads,

"...after a few days rest, the caravan proceeded onwards to Syria; and, on his return southwards, Hashim carried his bride with him to Mecca. As the days of her pregnancy advanced, she retired to her father's house at Medina, and there brought forth a son who, because

---

[9] www.muhammadspeaks.com/news.html

much white hair covered his infantile head, was called *Sheba* Al Hamd (Praise).

"After Hisham died, he left all of his wealth to Al Muttalib, his elder brother, one of Arabia's greatest entertainers. Meanwhile, his nephew, Sheba, was being raised by his widowed mother in the city of Medina, totally forgotten by his fathers powerful and rich relatives residing in Mecca.

Al Muttalib went to Medina seeking his brother son, Sheba. Upon finding him, he embraced and wept over him, and clothed him in a suit of Yemen raiment. His objective was take his nephew back to his fathers house in Mecca to restore his place among his father people. But, Al-Muttalib needed to appeal to his nephews mother wherein he explained, over a three-day time span, the great advantages her son was losing by absence from his father's house. Seeing him determined, she at last relented.[10]

Upon reaching Mecca, Al-Muttalib introduced Sheba to his countrymen, but they at first did not recognize the young lad. In fact, they inferred Al-Muttalib had purchased a slave until he exclaimed, "it is my nephew, Sheba, the son of Amr (Hashim.)" And as each scrutinized the features of the boy, they swore – "By my life! it is the very same." In this incident is said to have originated the name of ABD AL MUTTALIB, by which the son of Hashim was ever after called.[11]

---

[10] http://answering-islam.org/Books/Muir/Lifel/chapter4.htm

[11] Reference to Islamic history see http://answering-islam.org/Books/Muir/Lifel/chapter4.htm

In spite of recognizing the once lost and found Sheba, you read he was still identified by his uncles relatives as a slave. In addition, the next set of problems he faced was regaining the place and property of his father, **Hashim, whose name meant crusher of evil.**

In a 1962 Radio Broadcast, titled, "The Tribe of Shabazz" Elijah Muhammad delivered the following message, which capsulated the above history of Sheba Al Hamd. This Type  Antitype actually relates to the condition and restoration of the so-called American Negro. Mr. Muhammad addressed this subject in the following words:

"Greetings to you. I am Elijah Muhammad, the preacher of Freedom, Justice and Equality to the American so-called Negroes, the Lost and Found members of the Asiatic Black Nation and from The Tribe of Shabazz.

"The God of this people and of the Earth and of the heavens said that this man went into Africa, as it is known today in what they called at that time, the jungles of East Asia and began a tribe from himself because of the other scientists rejecting his idea. And the idea, I will not make it known on the air. But it is known, what his idea really was. And we are the people that he produced and that was 50,000 years ago, according to the Word of Almighty God, Allah, to me.

"There is also, according to the Holy Quran, and even according to His own sayings, a cycle of 50,000 years that once every 50,000 years, there comes a major change in our civilization. I say OUR civilization because that we had no other civilization on the Planet Earth, according to the Word of Almighty God, Allah, Who came in the Person of Master Fard Muhammad in the year 1930, here. I did not get acquainted with Him until 1931.

"And since 1931 after His Mission of me, I have been busy on this particular work of trying to resurrect my people into the knowledge of the presence of Almighty God, Whom the world has been looking for to come for the past 2,000 years. He is referred to in the 22nd Surah of the Quran as the Great Mahdi. Mahdi means one...according to the Quran... A Self-Independent Person--Guide that comes to guide others, while He, Himself, is self-guided. This is God In Person.

"So it was In the Person of Master Fard Muhammad. He referred to Himself as being Self-Independent. And that He came for our salvation. To put us on the right path, that we may be successful, referring to my people and myself -- the so-called American Negro."[12]

Many researchers have attempted to place a meaning to the origin and etymology of the name Sheba. This name according to Jones comparable with an Ethiopian word

---

[12] www.muhammadspeaks.com/shabazz.html

meaning 'man'. Jones reads Man. **BDB** (BDB: Brown-Driver-Briggs Hebrew and English Lexicon of the Old Testament) sees relations with a verb that means to make campaign or expedition, but lists סבא (*saba* 1455), which means to imbibe (see **Seba**). The name may even have to do with שבה (*shaba* 2311) to take captive.

שבא is used in the Aramaic Talmud to mean splinter, a possible derivative (says **BDB)** from the unused שבב(*shbb* 2309-2310), which yields שבבים(*shebabim* 2309a), splinters, and שביב(*shabib* 2310a), flame.[13]

Two of the operative words above is shebabim, splinter meaning broken off from a main body and Shaba meaing to take captive.

Islamic scholar, Mother Tynetta Muhammad, has stated Sheba is the feminine name for Shabazz. So in accordance to what Messenger Elijah Muhammad revealed in plain language, not only was Shabazz's history lost and forgotten after he left Mecca 50,000 years ago with his tribe,

---

[13] www.abarim-publications.com/Meaning/Sheba.html

but along with the meaning of that maternal name, Sheba, members of his tribe were ultimately captured by an enemy down the wheel of time. Consequently, his people served in servitude 400 years as slaves in the Western Hemisphere—North America. Fact is: Black America is a pedigree of one of Black Arabia's Priestly families.

By all observations, Mecca's secret history is mathematically congruent with what has recurred among the so-called American Negroes. Whether they know it or not, a certain measure of rehearsed Divine Acts of the Jews and Arabs of Mecca and Medina were Type Antitypes for Black America's deliverance. Such Divine Acts would not have been made known except for the coming of God in Person—the Great Mahdi of the Muslim world and Messiah of the Christians. His body was in deed prepared! He came at the end of a 50,000-year Quranic cycle {Holy Quran 70:4} *"A questioner may question the inevitable retribution. ²For the disbelievers, none can stop it. ³From GOD; Possessor of the highest Height. ⁴The angels, with their reports, climb to Him in* a day that equals 50,000 years. [5] Therefore, you shall resort to a gracious patience. [6] For they see it far away [7] While we see it very close." (Holy Quran 70:4)

Sheba Returns To Mecca

As the drama unfolded in Mecca, Abd al-Muttalib's (Shêba al-Hamd) relatives eventually had to come from Medina to Mecca to insure that the fatherless orphan's rights and property were restored according to Hashim's wishes.

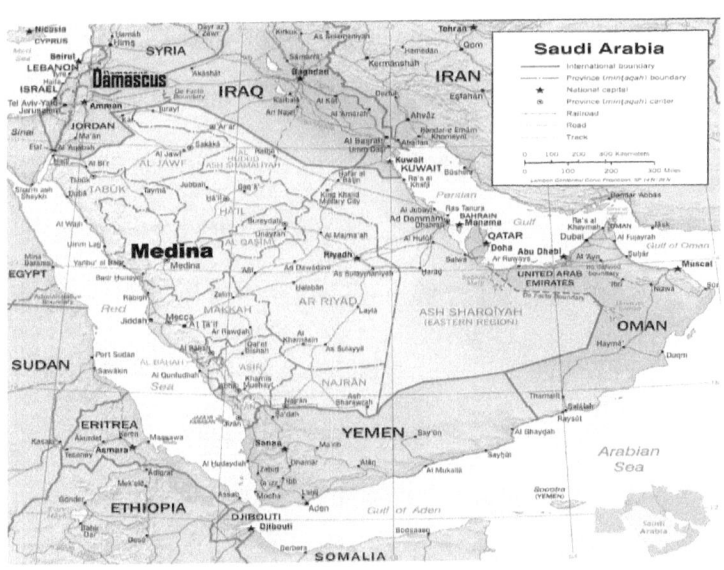

Medina; officially *(al-Madīnah al-Munawwarah)* is a city in the Hejaz region of western Saudi Arabia, and serves as the capital of the Al Madinah Province. It is the second holiest city in Islam. Medina is 210 mi (340 km) north of **Mecca** and about 120 mi (190 km) from the Red Sea coast.

To insure matters were corrected for Sheba, eighty members of his maternal relatives (Jewish side of his lineage) came to his aid. Of course, these Jews were not your everyday European Zionist Jews. They were the authentic Jews of the old world of Arabia. The first mention of Jews in the area of what is today Saudi Arabia dates back, by some accounts, to the time of the First Temple. By the 6th and 7th centuries there was a considerable Jewish population in Hejaz, mostly in and around Medina, in part because of the embrace of Judaism by such leaders as Dhu Nuwas. This man **Yūsuf Dhū Nuwas**, (Arabic: نــواس ذو يوســف) *ruled* 517 – 525 AD) was the last king of the Himyarite kingdom of Yemen and a convert to Judaism at time when Islam had not yet been revealed and established in Saudi Arabia.[14] Besides Arab

---

[14] http://en.wikipedia.org/wiki/Dhu_Nuwas

pagan religions, only Judaism and Christainity were available to those seeking worship.

Sheba's Rights Restored

The men whom had conspired to prevent Sheba from attaining his true position in Mecca were eventually daunted by the threat of death, and agreed to the concession, which was ratified by oath before the assembled Quraish.[15] In terms of rights to orphans, prophet Ezekiel wrote, *"In you they have had no respect for father and mother; in you they have been cruel to the man from a strange land; in you they have done wrong to the child without a father and to the widow." (Ezekiel 22:7)*

Therefore, what you have read thus far were signs of the history of the so-called American Negro hidden within the acts of the pedigree of Prophet Mohammed, his family lineage and how Allah took the acts of his family by employing them with the Divine Fulfillment of Time to Black America's history.

---

[15] Reference to Islamic history see http://answering-islam.org/Books/Muir/Life1/chapter4.htm

Farrakhan and the Jews

For anyone today to say Minister Farrakhan's appeal to the Jewish community to help restore Black America is off base is just purely ignorant of Divine History. Be it pre-Islamic or Islamic history or post Islamic history, the Type Antitype is in the here and now today! Deal with it because all of the cards are on the table for discussion that was once a hidden secret or a puzzle taken apart by Europe's religious God complex wealth class that were/are against the greatness and rise of the original Black Nation of the earth!

As it were, while meeting with Torah Jews, Minister Louis Farrakhan stated:

"Encouraging the rabbis to be more vocal in their opposition to  falsehood, Min. Farrakhan said America is being destroyed because of its moral degeneracy and the destruction of the family. He said only the family values taught in the Torah, Injil (Gospel) and the Holy Qur'an, "properly administered and fought for" will save America from a destruction that "will make Sodom and Gomorra ... look like child's play. "Satan is winning because the righteous are divided and are weak. Sometimes the righteous are cowardly in that we are afraid to stand up for God so He can prove that even though we are small in number, He will make us prevail over armies as He showed you the history of the Children of Israel," he said.

"We do not believe that Jesus of 2000 years ago was the Messiah. We believe the Messiah was yet to come, and this is the time period that the Messiah would make himself manifest," Min. Farrakhan said.

"He added that his teacher, the Hon. Elijah Muhammad, told his followers to study the history of the Jewish people because it is full of lessons for Blacks in America who have suffered a 400-year bondage "unlike the slavery of other human beings. After 400 years, (God) gave them Moses, the liberator," he said. "And we, too, believe that Allah has been merciful to us and it is our time now to come out of exile, but it is also your time as well. We believe that Elijah, who was to come before that great and dreadful day of the Lord ... has come into the world, not only to turn our hearts back to our fathers, but to turn the hearts of the people of the Book, who have strayed from the path of God, turn them back, because only in turning us back to the path of God can we truly come out of exile and again be called the people of God," he said.

Today's Jews have only been invited to help restore the members of the lost and found Tribe of Shabazz/Sheba. It is not that Allah is depending upon them to do so. However, it is in their own best interest to participate as they (European Jews) participated in the Atlantic slave trade and other financial schemes, which made it succeed for 310 years. For more concrete information about European Jewish involvement with slavery, read *The Secret Relationship Between Blacks and Jews* Vol. 1 and Vol. 2.

The question is not about anti-Semitism. The Question is: Is the Jewish Talmud Anti-Black and Anti-Christian? ACCORRDING TO DEMETRIC MUHAMMAD-FCN GUEST COLUMNIST,...There is a tiny Jewish sect who makes considerable effort to eschew the *Talmud* and adhere to the Torah alone. These are the Karaites, a group which, historically, has been most hated and severely persecuted by the orthodox Jewish rabbinate. The Ethiopian Jews have no knowledge of the *Talmud,* as it is the product of European Jewry.

The *Talmud* is not the Torah. The Torah is also known as the Old Testament of the Christian Bible. The Talmud purports to be a Rabbinical Commentary on the Torah for the purpose of guiding every aspect of Jewish life. The most revered is known as the Babylonian Talmud. It is a book that contains 4500 pages of the opinions of leading Jewish Rabbis. It is viewed as a holy writing and it is closely guarded.[16]

For your more background about Talmud, read these modern scholarly works.

- Y. N. Epstein, *Mevo-ot le-Sifrut haTalmudim*
- Hanoch Albeck, *Mavo la-talmudim*
- Louis Jacobs, "How Much of the Babylonian Talmud is Pseudepigraphic?" Journal of Jewish Studies 28, No. 1 (1977), pp. 46–59
- Saul Lieberman, *Hellenism in Jewish Palestine* (New York: Jewish Theological Seminary, 1950)
- Jacob Neusner, *Sources and Traditions: Types of Compositions in the Talmud of Babylonia* (Atlanta: Scholars Press, 1992).
- David Weiss Halivni, *Mekorot u-Mesorot* (Jerusalem: Jewish Theological Seminary, 1982 on)
- Yaakov Elman, "Order, Sequence, and Selection: The Mishnah's Anthological Choices," in David Stern, ed. *The Anthology in Jewish Literature* (Oxford: Oxford University Press, 2004) 53-80
- Strack, Herman L. and Stemberger, Gunter, *Introduction to the Talmud and Midrash*, tr. Markus Bockmuehl: repr. 1992, hardback ISBN 978-0-567-09509-1, paperback ISBN 978-0-8006-2524-5
- Moses Mielziner, *Introduction to the Talmud*: repr. 1997, hardback ISBN 978-0-8197-0156-5, paperback ISBN 978-0-8197-0015-5
- Aviram Ravitzky, *Aristotelian Logic and Talmudic Methodology* (Hebrew): Jerusalem 2009, ISBN 978-965-493-459-6

---

[16] http://www.finalcall.com/artman/publish/Perspectives_1/article_7291.shtml

Chapter III

Well of Zam Zam

Although Sheba, whose new name became Abd al Muttalib after returning to Mecca from Medina, was now acknowledge by a ratified oath from certain leaders of Mecca, and succeeded to the office of entertaining the pilgrims for a long time. Yet, he was destitute of power and influence. So once again, we can see similar traits about Sheba (Abd al Muttalib) the entertainer having no power and influence just like the Black Nation of America—the worlds greatest entertainers, yet destitute of true power and influence.

What turned Abd al Muttalib's fortune around was discovering the ancient Well of Zam Zam. What is the Well of Zam Zam? It is an endless underground water supply buried beneath the Desert sands of Mecca, Arabia. It was choked up either accidentally or by design, and the remembrance of it was so indistinct that the site was unknown until Abd al Muttalib (Shêba al-Hamd) uncovered it. History says he and his son Harith dug deeper and deeper into the sand, and also came upon the two golden gazelles, with the swords and suits of armour buried there by the Jorhomite king more than 300 years before.[17]

This occurred when all other wells in Mecca were abandoned until Abd al Muttalib (Shêba al-Hamd) at last discovered one and began supplying water for pilgrims who visited the Holy City Mecca. When ask how he found the Well, he explained that it came to him in his mind through a series four dreams directing him to Zamzam's location. Thereafter his wealth and great responsibility as the supplier of water to pilgrims increased. Subsequently, his need for a large family of powerful sons became necessary.

Envy Toward The Man With Wealth And Knowledge

Envy toward Abd al Muttalib's fame and wealth reached various tribes throughout the Arabian Peninsula; namely, the house of Umayyad, but the leader of this tribe

---

[17] Reference to Islamic history see http://answering-islam.org/Books/Muir/Lifel/chapter4.htm

proved to be less superior then Sheba (Abd al Muttalib) and his ten sons. Until today, 1,400 years later, ill feelings between the two branches continue. Hence, one reason the founder of the Nation of Islam in the West, Master W. Fard Muhammad, did not create the lost and found Nation of Islam to subject themselves to the old Islamic world leadership, religious scholarship and exegesis.[18]

Although the lost Black Nation in America is mainly this world greatest entertainers, yet destitute of power and influence, Allah (God) has placed among them a mental Well of Zam Zam. He has placed this principle in the mind of the Honorable Louis Farrakhan Muhammad and his helpers.

The old world of Islam became a house divided centuries ago. Fact is the British government took control over Arabian politics between 1930 or 1931. Nevertheless, ancient Islamic Type Antitype events were employed and fulfilled in North America by the ongoing restoration process

---

[18] **Exegesis** (from the Greek ξήγησις from ξηγε σθαι 'to lead out') is a critical explanation or interpretation of a text, especially a religious text.

of America's former slaves whether they knew what was going on or not {Psalms 118:23} *"This is the LORD'S doing; it is wonderful in our eyes."*

I recall first meeting face to face with the Minister in 1981. We were drinking a cup of coffee downtown San Diego, California. The brother whom I had accompanied to the meeting was Harvey J. X Robinson. At a certain point during the meeting, I asked Minister Farrakhan to teach me about Egypt. After he looked into my eyes with a very serious expression, he said "first read all of the Messengers books, and then I will teach you about Egypt." Of Course, I went straight way to read all of his books. It is my belief that after reading Message To The Blackman in America, The Fall of America, Our Saviour Has Arrived, The Flag of Islam, How To Eat to Live VOL. 1 and 2, plus the many lectures Delivered by Messenger Muhammad's best helper, Minister Louis Farrakhan, the Well of Zam Zam opened. For the Well of Zam Zam spiritually represents the Divine Wisdom of God buried in every man, women and child. To find it means get knowledge and search within self too!

Chapter IV

19 x 30 =570

The child given the name SHEBA at birth ultimately comes to age and is renamed Abd al Muttalib. Of his ten sons, one of them became known as Prophet Mohammed. He was born in Mecca 570 or (571 AD - Madina 632). The central messenger and prophet in Islam; the receiver and transmitter of Gods Quranic message to mankind. His father named him Mohammed Ibn Abdullah, which means Mohammed, son of Abdullah.

Coincidentally, if we decoded the year, 570 AD, of Prophet Mohammed's birth by its two multiplying factors, that will be 19 x 30 which equals 570. Simply put: Master Fard Muhammad founded the Nation of Islam in the West in 1930, hence we see 19 x 30 = 570 as pointed out by Mother Tynetta Muhammad. What is being exposed by these numbers is Wealth and Riches that shall come to the Black man and women of America who shall be employed throughout the ends of the earth for good and prosperity with wealth and riches.

To say it clearly and simply, the chief rulers of the policies deployed by the white race of mankind have ruined their people's covenant with God in Person. Historically and presently, their sin is very grievous; [Gen 18.20], wicked and ungodly [Gen 18.23]. On a historical scale, their politics have been vile and horrid especially toward darker skin people of the earth and God in Person has Condemn their entire rule. Of course, this does not mean darker skinned nations are exonerated from the Judgment. However, it does mean after the Judgment a new ruler will be established over the current world rulers.

But, I digress. Getting back to the reason for this mathematical sign in the numbers 19 x 30 = 570 is because God's language is mathematics and mathematics is Islam. For all practical intent and purpose, the secret history of Mecca and Arabia's divine family lineage is congruent with the execution of a plan carried out in North America by the Great

Mahdi—God in Person and the circle of Islamic Scientists who prepared Him.

"In Sunni Islam, the doctrine of the Mahdi has been questioned by some theologians. There is no explicit reference to the Mahdi in either the Qur'an or Sahih al-Bukhari, the most trusted collection of hadith in Sunni Islam; however, each of the remaining five collections of hadith, which together with Sahih al-Bukhari constitute the six canonical collections of hadith, does refer to the Mahdi. Even among those Sunni Muslims that accept the Mahdi doctrine, there is disagreement on the timing and nature of his advent and guidance."[19]

The Jews refer to this one as the Holy One of Israel because of His mother. Her Type Antitype was also connected to Prophet Mohammed's family lineage through his uncle Hashim and his marriage to the daughter of Amr, a Khazrajite of the Bani Najjar, one of the Jewish tribes of Arabia.

According to the Nation of Islam, the Type Antitype of Prophet Mohammed's family history lineage, including the history of Bilal, although many details were "cut out" from what is written within the 114 Quranic chapters and hadith, such history is clarified and correlates with what has

---

[19] en.wikipedia.org/wiki/Mahdi

occurred among America's former slaves exactly how Allah planned it thousands of years ago.

Then with the birth of Prophet Mohammed and the events throughout his family lineage, we have a foreshadow for the preparation of The Holy One that came from Mecca seeking to save and to restore the lost members of the tribe of Shabazz. Messenger Elijah Muhammad taught this in plain language to many a generation before today, but who believed his report {Isaiah 53:1} *"Who hath believed our report? and to whom is the arm of the LORD revealed?"* You ask who revealed what He revealed to Elijah Muhammad, it was Al-Mahdi—God in the Personage of Master W. Fard Muhammad.

Al-Mahdi Is God in Person

Mecca's ancient secret is that Allah (God) has always been a Person—the Black man of Asia, sons of men, but not your run-in-mills. Always their has been a Supreme Being in the mist of men whom no one knew for trillions of years until He made Himself known to the first begotten of the dead. Not in 570 AD but in the year 1931. To get a *not so spooky* understanding into this expression, *first-begotten of the dead*, study the Greek expression - **πρωτότοκος prōtotokos**, which occurs in Bible Colossians 1:18.

It turns out by all accounts, as one Islamic scholar, Dr. Wesley Muhammad, actually makes obvious: Allah (God) is a person and always has been according to Quranic language. His research into the word Al-Ghaib, particularly, in Quranic terminology, describes the presence of Allah as a man or anthropomorphic being. Although most modern Islamic scholars say ghaib simply means "unseen" and attach its meaning as incorporeity (immateriality), Dr. Wesley Muhammad elaborates: "**the word 'Al-Ghaib' means to 'withdraw ones presence from; absence from view' denoting 'a being that can be seen but has made a conscious decision to withdraw his presence until the appoint hour...'**"[20]

On the other hand, the Honorable Elijah Muhammad clarified this subject too. In plain language he said,

[20] http://www.theblackgod.com/The%20Great%20Debate.pdf

"The Bible mentions Him as the Son of Man and also mentions Him as not being a man but a spirit. On one side He is made clear and on the other He is made a mystery. Representation such as this causes confusion in understanding. We are blind to the knowledge of God when we make Him a mystery and unreal.

"Anyone so blind to the reality of God is the servant of the devil, until he or she sees God as a reality. Thousands of years the devil has been blinding man to God's reality, and that is the reason why God had to come in person (and He has), to clear us of such ignorance and blindness to the knowledge of Him.

"Therefore, we have the "Coming of Allah (God)." He is referred to as the Son of Man because, first, He is the Son of Man and gotten for a special purpose, which is to return the lost back to their own and to punish and destroy the wicked for their destruction of the righteous, that the righteous may live in peace and do the will of the God of righteousness, free from trouble and interference. Second, He must be a man to deal with man, and we cannot receive or respect other than man.

"Since His work is to destroy the wicked. He must remain hidden from the eyes of the world until the time is ripe (the end), for the two (God and devil) cannot rule together.

"The Son of man (Allah) must wait until His time, after the works of the devil. (II Thessalonians 2:8-9; Holy Qur'an 7:14-18). And another place in the Holy Qur'an describes them as the people with the blue eyes. Holy Qur'an 20:102).[21]

When Muslims say Al-Mahdi, it is the Son of Man according to the language of the Christian. His birth pedigree is linked (Type Antitype) to the lineage of Prophet Mohammed

---

[21] Excerpt from "Message to the Blackman," 1965.

Ibn Abdullah—a mixture of the Asiatic Blacks and Semitic tribes of Arabia. In other words, the black and the white or as the Arabs would say, the black and red. (See appendix 1 Black and Semitic)

Al-Mahdi is a title to denote a self-guided one. This self-guided one was born in the Holy Mecca, Arabia. One of the names He used after publicly introducing Himself to Black America in 1930 was W. D. Fard when He began initiating Islam to the lost and found members of the Tribe of Shabazz in the West. Then in 1931 when a former sharecropper from Georgia named ELIJAH POOLE [Muhammad] first visited the Temple of Islam in Detroit, Michigan, he said to FARD:

"Who are you, and what is your real name?' He said, 'I am the one that the world has been expecting for the past 2,000 years.' I said to him again, 'What is your name?' He said, 'My name is Mahdi; I am God, I came to guide you into the right path that you may be successful and see the hereafter.' He described the destruction of the world with bombs, poison gas, and finally fire that would consume and destroy everything of the present world.

"Not anything of it (the present world of white mankind) would be left. Those escaping the destruction would not be allowed to carry anything of it out with them....

"...He used the name Wallace D. Fard often signing it W.D. Fard. In the third year (1933). He signed his name W.F. Muhammad, which stands for Wallace Fard Muhammad. He came alone. He began teaching us the knowledge of ourselves, of God and the devil, the measurement of the earth, other planets and the civilization of some of the planets other than Earth."[22]

Furthermore, He described Black people as His uncle in terms of the lineage connection (Type Antitype) between Black America and their righteous brethren who once ruled the Holy City Mecca. He wrote in brief:

"1.   My name is W. F. M U H A M M A D.
2.   I came to North America by myself.
3.   My uncle was brought over here by the Trader three hundred seventy-nine years ago.
4.   My uncle cannot talk his own language.
5.   He does not know that he is my uncle."[23]

By unraveling the Arabian lineage connection, in real time, the nephew, W. F. Muhammad, came to North America to retrieve and restore his uncle, Elijah Muhammad. Recall, during the days of Al Muttalib, he went to Medina to retrieve and restore his nephew Sheba al-Hamd (Abd al Muttalib). As

[22] http://www.muhammadspeaks.com/PitttsburghCourier5-26-1959.html
[23] www.thenationofislam.org/englishlesson.html

one might notice, in last days of the resurrection of the dead, the rolls were reversed—the uncle (Tribe of Shabazz) was lost and needed to be found rather than the nephew (Sheba al Hamd).

As it were, the secret history of Mecca contained some keys employed by Al-Mahdi and His father that prepared a body to come among a white ruled country, America, to make Muslims out of so-called Negroes, America's former slaves. The first Muslim He made was Elijah Muhammad.

[3]Then Jesus told them this parable: [4]"Suppose one of you has a hundred sheep and loses one of them. Does he not leave the ninety-nine in the open country and go after the lost sheep until he finds it? [5]And when he finds it, he joyfully puts it on his shoulders [6]and goes home.... (Luke 15:3-6)

Lineage of Jesus

Jewish and Christian religious scientists explain the lineage of Jesus according to their interpretation of prophecy. They say Jesus had to be born in the line of David according to 2 Samuel 7:12-13. Referring to David, these verses say, *"When your days are over and you rest with your fathers, I will raise up your offspring to succeed you, who will come from your own body, and I will establish his kingdom. He is the one who will build a house for my Name, and I will establish the throne of his kingdom forever.*" The Davidic line reaches through the line of Seth to Noah, through the line of Shem to Abraham. Then through the lines of Isaac, Jacob, Judah, David, and to Jesus.

The lineage of Jesus is recorded in two places: Matthew 1:1-17 and Luke 3:28-38. It seems as if these two genealogies of Jesus contradict. Do they? Most biblical scholars assume that Luke is referring to the genealogy of Mary and that the genealogy recorded in Matthew is of Joseph. The Matthew genealogy follows Joseph's line (Jesus' legal father), through David's son Solomon. Luke follows Mary's line (Jesus' blood mother), through David's son Nathan. Through both of these lines, Jesus Christ is David's descendant and is eligible to be the promised Messiah.

Tracing a genealogy through the mother's line is somewhat unusual, but the virgin birth is unusual as well![24]

Although Jewish and Christian scholars have explained a few details about the birth Jesus 2,000 years ago, much confusion still surrounds his birth and genetic family lineage. What they have been trying to hide is the original Black genetic side of Jesus' nature and family lineage, just as today's white Arabs have hidden the Black genetic side of Prophet Mohammed's nature and family lineage.

Muslims know Jesus as Isa bin Yusef (Jesus son of Joseph) and/or Isa bin Maryam (Jesus son of Mary). I reiterate, hidden beneath this mans family lineage and the family lineage of Prophet Mohammed were signs of the actual birth of the Divine Supreme Being or the Great Mahdi, the Son of Man—God in Person. He founded the Nation of Islam (N.O.I.) from 1930 to 1934. By the time He departed, there were

---

[24] www.allaboutjesuschrist.org/lineage-of-jesus-faq.htm

25,000 registered N.O.I. members. His light and *newborn* Nation had indeed risen in the west!

In 2010, some never the wiser may argue, "If FARD Muhammad is "all that" why aren't all Black people registered in the Nation of Islam today. Simply put:

"6. He likes the Devil because the Devil gives him nothing.
7. Why does he like the Devil?
8. Because the Devil put fear in him when he was a little boy.
9. Why does he fear, now, since he is a big man?
10. Because the Devil taught him to eat the wrong food.
11. Does that have anything to do with the above question, No. 10?
12. Yes, sir! That makes him other than his own self.
13. What is his own self?
14. His own self is a righteous Muslim.
15. Are there any Muslims other than righteous?
16. I beg your pardon? I have never heard of one.
17. How many Muslim sons are there in North America?
18. Approximately three million.
19. How many original Muslims are there in North America?
20. A little over seventeen million.
21. Did I hear you say that some of the seventeen million do not know that they are Muslims?
22. **YES, SIR!**
23. I hardly believe that unless they are blind, deaf and dumb.
24. Well, they were made blind, deaf and dumb by the Devil when they were babies.
25. **CAN THE DEVIL FOOL A MUSLIM?**
26. **NOT NOWADAYS,**

27. Do you mean to say that the Devil fooled then three hundred seventy-nine years ago?

28. Yes, the **T R A D E R** made an interpretation that they receive **G O L D** for their labor - more than they were earning in their own country.

29. Then did then receive gold?

30. **NO.** The Trader disappeared and there was no one that could speak their language.

31. Then what happened?

32. **WELL,** they wanted to go to their own country, but they could not swim nine thousand miles.

33. Why didn't their own people come and get them?

34. Because their own people did not know that they were here.

35. When did their own people find out that they were here?

36. Approximately sixty years ago.

After accomplishing this Lesson No. C1, at once ask for Lesson No. C2 which will bring you a profit of $10.00 per word for studying it."[25]

This particular lesson ABOVE was written by Master Fard Muhammad for all registered Muslims to study and memorize. He left this among the N.O.I. in 1934. Those members who had first access to these lessons as well as five other lessons prepared by FARD assisted Him in founding the N.O.I. His foremost assistant, however, was none other than the Honorable Elijah Muhammad (HEM). Yet, millions have refused

---

[25] http://www.thenationofislam.org/englishlesson.html

to see HEM and the True Master for fear of the devil, envy and rebellion.

"Jesus said to him, "Have I been with you all this time, Philip, and you still do not know me? The person who has seen me has seen the Father. So how can you say, 'Show us the Father'? (John 14:9)

As you may have comprehended by the verse above, Jesus was in the mist of his people, yet some did not recognize his work. Therefore, Phillip is given as a Type Antitype that applies to then as well as now for never the wiser.

Chapter V

Son of Islam Rises In The West

Both Quranic prophecy and Bible prophecy indicated God in Person, Al-Mahdi, or Son of Man would come from the east to the west to seek and save His lost people and raise a Messenger from among them.

"Abu Hurayra (R.A.) narrated ... that the Messenger of Allah SWT said: "The day of the hour will not come until the sun rises from the west, if it rises and the people saw it they will all believe, when a time where nothing will be accepted anymore of believe the truth"

Of course, the foolish and ignorant take this to mean the physical sun could rise from the western skies. But the Bible says it like this:

"For as lightning that comes from the east is visible even in the west, so will be the coming of the Son of Man." (Matthew 24:27)

This prophecy was fulfilled in 1930 as mentioned earlier. The other factors relate to the second spiritual rise of Minister Farrakhan who had finally earned leadership over the Nation of Islam after it was other thrown in 1975 by the

U.S. government, et al. Thereafter, it took FARRAKHAN two years to realize and fulfill his part of Quranic history in the Western world. His rise to leadership over the Nation of Islam began in 1977 represented a second spiritual Islamic resurrection for Black America because in general they had rebelled under the leadership of Elijah Muhammad during his first 40-years among them as the Messenger of Allah from 1934-35 to 1975. Hence, the Quran says,

[104]And We said thereafter to the Children of Israel, 'Dwell securely in the land (of promise)': but when the second of the warnings came to pass, We gathered you together in a mingled crowd. [105]We sent down the (Qur'an) in Truth, and in Truth has it descended: and We sent thee but to give Glad Tidings and to warn (sinners). [106](It is) a Qur'an which We have divided (into parts from time to time), in order that thou mightest recite it to men at intervals: We have revealed it by stages." (Holy Quran 17:104-106)

Minister Louis Farrakhan's raise to leadership occurred during the second resurrection of the Nation of Islam, as it were, represents the Type Antitype to the above Quranic history. Although he registered in the Nation of Islam in 1955, first spiritual resurrection, his second spiritual resurrection occurred in 1977 at the farthest horizon in North

America i.e., the West Coast, Los Angeles, California. What happened on the West coast in 1977 *(or 30 months after the departure of Elijah Muhammad in 1975)* was the answer to a prayer hidden in the 27th sura (Chapter) of the Holy Quran verse 30. Written in this verse is what is called an extra Bismillah (prayer), which is 19 Quranic Chapters away from where it was not written i.e., Chapter 9. Bismillah means In the name of Allah—the prayer every Muslim makes before any very important situation or event.

"27:30 The `Basmalah' [Bismillah] included in this verse compensates for the `Basmalah' that is missing from Sura 9, **19 suras earlier**.... Every sura in the Quran opens with the statement **"In the name of God, Most Gracious, Most Merciful,"** known as the Basmalah [Bismillah], with the exception of Sura 9... But the absence of the Basmalah from Sura 9 causes the number of this crucial opening statement to be 113, a number that does not conform with the Quran's code. However, we find that this deficiency is compensated for in Sura 27. Two Basmalahs...From the missing Basmalah of Sura 9 to the extra Basmalah of Sura 27, there are 19 suras....The occurrence of the extra Basmalah in 27:30 conforms with the Quran's code..."[26]

---

[26] www.submission.org/suras/app29.html

In view of mathematical science provided above, a second chance was given to a rebellious lost people to submit to Islam. The timing of FARRAKHAN'S rise was not by chance. Master W. Fard Muhammad taught His Messenger, Elijah Muhammad, what to do to ensure FARRAKHAN would fulfill the answer to a prayer so that the **son of Islam** would rise in the West, which is where Muhammad Mosque #27 was established! His rise took place on the West Coast where Elijah Muhammad sent Bernard E. X Moore (aka Jabril Muhammad) during the early 1950's and four other brothers from New York to lay the ground, although unbeknownst to any of them.

Interview With Emeritus A. Wazir Muhammad

According the oldest living West Coast Minister in the Nation of Islam, *Emeritus* Wazir Muhammad, he said "when Bro. Jabril was brought to L.A. [along with Malcolm X] we didn't have a [temple] number then but it was the fastest growing [temple] in the nation at that time.... What had happened, there was a brother named Thomas J. who went to

72

San Diego and asked Min. Majied, the Minister of [Temple] #8, which was the first [temple] on the west coast, to come down. [Bro. Thomas] was having meetings in his home and [things] spread fast enough to the point where we had secured – not we, because I wasn't a Muslim then, matter of fact, I was in jail as usual – but they were having meetings in the house and it was very successful. They started meeting first over on Washington in the theater, after that, they had the Masonic Hall which was on Normandy and Jefferson.... When we got that hall, Bro. Malcolm started coming and all those brothers came together and formed the foundation of the temple]. It was growing so fast that Malcolm brought five brothers from New York to help us get organized and get the temple established. Out of those five, Bro. Jabril – who at that time was Bernard E. X, slave name Moore – he was brought to become the secretary. There was a brother named Henry who was out of [Temple] #7 and he was the minister; a brother named Larry was [the] captain, and two

73

other brothers: Adam D., who was a teacher and I can't remember the other brother's name....

"Was it Malcolm's decision to bring the five from N.Y. or did he have to clear that through Elijah Muhammad? Wazir Muhammad states: 'I'm certain he cleared it because Malcolm's dedication and obedience to Elijah Muhammad is not the kind of thing that is portrayed by the media. [He] was a very devoted and very obedient person in the work that he did. He got the wisdom to do it from Elijah Muhammad; the way to do, what to do and all of that. He was just an executor of the kinds of things that Allah sent him to do. He more or less went around the country working, setting up and organizing [temples] – this is the kind of work he was doing. Everything he did, he did it in the name of Elijah Muhammad....

"Although Bro. Jabril was not brought to be the minister, he had a greater knowledge of Islam, he knew the program. He knew The Honorable Elijah Muhammad's word and that it was in fact the source of what we were about so he studied it very well. We didn't have books but he had gotten Elijah Muhammad's articles out of the Pittsburgh Courier Newspaper. He showed us how to study and get Elijah Muhammad's word so that when we started reading Quran and Bible we would really understand what it was because the understanding was in understanding the word of Elijah Muhammad....Because of the knowledge that [Bro. Jabril] had, the people who emerged as the laborers, who consequently are responsible for the Islam that was established out on the West Coast, all of them gravitated to him. Bro. Henry was a wonderful brother and a good speaker but he did not have the knowledge of Islam as Bro. Jabril did.... We all became one group and Allah allowed us to be able to establish Islam then. We were under Muhammad's [Temple] of Islam...

"[At one point,] I went with [Bro. Jabril] the first lecture he delivered in Riverside [Ca.] and the title was "The Coming of the Son of Man" and he took about four hours. To this day I've never witnessed such a well organized – he tried to be so much in depth and when [the people] left there, everybody was crazy because Elijah Muhammad had written a series, "The Coming of the Son of Man," in the Pittsburgh Courier. [Bro. Jabril] studied those articles and had the thing organized. We're talking so far back [but] that's something I'll never forget... Riverside, San Bernadino and Empire had been problematic since the beginning. As a tactic of Elijah Muhammad, the way he spread Islam from coast to coast and border to border, he put 52 articles in the Amsterdam News [in N.Y.] and that covered the East coast. He put 52 [of the] same articles in the Herald Dispatch Newspaper [in L.A.] and that covered the West coast. He filled America with sunshine and Jabril planted Islam in the manner he saw his leader do it....

"I [became a minister] in '61 and the temple was attacked in '62 and I was sent to jail for defending the [temple] in '65. After I came out of jail in '66, I had a chance to be with Elijah Muhammad.

"...Bro. Jabril, he was the minister in Phoenix [by now] and when [Elijah Muhammad] wanted to get out of Chicago or Cleveland, that's where he would come."[27]

And so it was in Phoenix, Arizona where the Honorable Elijah Muhammad be preparing Minister Jabril Muhammad with the wherewithal to seek and to get FARRAKHAN at the appropriate moment in time to answer the call to a prayer in Holy Quran 27:30-.31.

[30] *"It is from Solomon, and is (as follows): '**In the name of Allah, Most Gracious, Most Merciful:*** [31] *"'[Sheba] Be ye not arrogant against me, but come to me in submission (to the true Religion).'"*

Unbeknownst to Minister Farrakhan (Louis X Walcott) back in the 1955 did he think one day he'd be leading the Nation of Islam approximately 19 years or so from the time when he was given his first official post by Messenger Muhammad. According to history, after receiving his "basic training," Min. Malcolm X under the guidance of the Honorable

[27] http://bhonline.org/blog/?tag=jabril-muhammad-bernard-cushmeer

Elijah Muhammad dispatched the then-Louis X to Boston to serve as captain, the coordinator of men's affairs. Soon thereafter, he was elevated to the post of minister in 1956-57 at Muhammad's Temple No. 11.[28]

Without going any further, the mathematics speaks for itself i.e., the number 19, the number 27, and the number 30 all play into the intrigue details of the Quranic mathematics from chapter 9 to 27 v. 30 and the meeting between FARRAKHAN and JABRIL.

Appendix 2 will provide the Type Antitype of the relationship between prophet Mohammed and the Jabrill, the angel with their subset antitypes Minister Farrakhan and Minister Jabril in Los Angeles, California 1977. (See Appendix 2 Explanation of Hadith Jibrill)

Summary

In summary, black men and women of America as well as 9/10th of the original people of the earth have been bombarded with a Caucasian version of who God is and how

---

[28] www.finalcall.com/national/savioursday2k/farrakhan.htm

God's prophecies apply to mankind. Aboriginal human beings have been taught mainly about biblical Caucasian saints, prophets and holy people by the Western world religious scholars.

Therefore, provided in this book, *Secrets of The Holy City Mecca, Arabia* are genealogical facts about an Asiatic lineage of Black people from the holy land whose time has come to be properly incorporated into their true Type Antitype accord by divine light of history. This light ranges from tribes to angels to God Himself

One has been especially prepared—genetically made of both people, white and black, who came out of Mecca, Arabia by Himself to end the old world and bring into reality the new world. Although He is made of both people, the foundation He stands upon is an ancient foundation designed by the originator of the heavens and earth whose secrets and wisdom of the ages will not be defeated.

"Behold, [although] I have willed to keep it hidden, the Last Hour is bound to come, so that every human being may be recompensed in accordance with what he strove for [in life]. {Holy Quran 20:15}

"No one knows when his time will come. Like fish that are caught in a cruel net or birds caught in a snare, humans are trapped by a disaster when it suddenly strikes them." (Ecclesiastes 9:12)

Semites verses Blacks

Gradually many of the Semitic Arabs were compelled to surrender to the wisdom and cultural superiority of their Black neighbors and were forced to adhere to the Yemenite LAW and adapt Yemenite language and custom. Some subversive factions chafed under foreign rule and were a source of social unrest and upheaval. In time through as portion of the Semites became an integral part of the cultural fabric of this mixed Arab society. The gradual amalgamation of these Red Arabs with the original Black Arabs produced a more culturally refined and civilized Semite. This physiognomical blending also resulted in the development of a darker skinned Semite with a slender yet muscular build. Uthman Amr Ibn Bahr Al-Jahiz, renowned Islamic, 'in 860 CE commented on this race mixing: [said], When they [Blacks] mixed with our group, they were said to be tan and brownish-black...and their name was derived from ours, at a time when we were the only ones to be called Blacks. They [Semites] must not be called Blacks unless they are from us'.

The debut of this dark Semite on the Arabian stage caused a change in 'attitude toward the Blacks who had led them from the darkness of barbarism into the light of civilization. Such is the testimony of the historians in antiquity: *The Semitic Arabs take pride in blackness of color'*...This new perspective on black was not held by all Semitic Arab tribes and families; many chose to remain *'in cultural stagnation to live and die by the sword'*. This group of Semitics continued to look upon the Arabian Blacks with distain and malice.

The next change in the relations between Arabian Blacks and Red Semitics was a result of another pivotal population shift. Black families in the north began to return to their ancestral homes in Yemen and the balance of power rotated again from north to south. The northern Black fortifications were weakened and, eventually, the Semites gained control in the early sixth century and, putting into practice what they had learned from the Yemenites, established the first Semitic hierarchy in Arabia's northern plateau.[29]

[29] African Presence in Early Asia, by Runoko Rashidi and co-edited by Ivan Van Sertima: Pg. 276-278 (1985)

Appendix 1

Explanation of Angel Jabril

The Explanation of Hadith Jibril About Belief ('Iman)

الحَمْدُ لله ربِّ العالمينَ لهُ النِّعمة وله الفضلُ ولهُ الثَّناءُ الحسن صلواتُ اللهِ البَرِّ الرحيم والملائكةِ المُقرَّبينَ بِه مِنَ النَّبِيينَ والمُرسلينَ وءال كلِّ على سيِّدِنا مُحَمَّدٍ أشرفِ المرسلينَ وحبيبِ ربِّ العالمينَ وعلى جميع إخوانِ وسلامُ الله عليهمْ أجمعينَ والصَّالحينَ.

من أتى مسجدًا وكان هَمُهُ أن يَتَعَلَّمَ أو يُعَلِّمَ خيرًا " :أمَّا بعدُ، فقد وَرَدَ في الحديثِ عن النبيّ عَلَيه الصلاةُ والسلام "كانَ له أجرُ حَج وَعُمرَةٍ تامين.

هذا الأمرُ يُعطيهِ اللهُ لمن قصد موضعًا نيَّتُهُ أن يتعلم الخير أو يُعَلِّمَ الخير، والعلمُ، علم الدين واسعٌ جدًا إنما أهم الأمور تعلمًا وتعليمًا هو الاعتناء بعقيدة أهلُ السُّنَّةِ والجماعةِ وهو عند الله مهمًا جدًا، لذلك قال العلماءُ يجب على .لم الواجبات من علم الدِّين ويجب عليه أن يعلمها لغيرهالإنسان أن يتع

Praise be to Allah the Lord of the worlds, to Him belongs the Everlastingness and the befitting attributes. May Allah raise the rank and increase the honor of our great Prophet Muhammad *sallallahu ^alayhi wa sallam* and protect his Muslim nation from that which he fears for it.

Thereafter, it was reported in the hadith of the Prophet [Mohammed]... said:

It means: "The one who comes to a mosque and his concern is to learn or teach the goodness of the Religion,

84

would earn a reward similar to the reward of performing a complete Hajj (Pilgrimage) and ^Umrah."

This reward is given to the one who goes to a place with the intention to teach or learn the goodness of the Religion. The Knowledge of the Religion is very vast and the most important matter, whether to learn or teach, is to take good care of the Creed of Ahlus-Sunnah wal Jama^ah. This Knowledge is very important to Allah and that is why the scholars said it is obligatory on the person to learn the obligatory matters of the Religion and to teach them to others.

It was mentioned in the hadith, which is known as the hadith of Jibril, that while the Prophet was with his Companions, a man came and joined their session. His clothes were so white and his hair was extremely black and did not have the appearance of a traveling person. In fact that was Jibril, who came in the shape of a man to teach the Companions the matters of the Religion. Among the things which Jibril asked the Prophet was: 'Tell me about 'Iman (Belief).'

The Prophet... said it means: 'To believe in Allah, His Angels, His Revealed Books, His Messengers, the Last Day, and to believe in destiny (qadar)--both good and evil...'

Moreover, the angels love to descend to the circles of Knowledge, Allah ta^ala orders them to descend to the circles of Knowledge, they would bring mercy to these circles and ask Allah to forgive those who are attending them; that is why the person who goes many times to the circles of Knowledge feels some change in his status. Attending the circles of Knowledge is a blessing; one does not know its value until the Day of Judgment. So do not miss this opportunity; the Messenger of Allah *sallallahu alayhi wa sallam* said:[30]

---

[30] www.alsunna.org/The-Explanation-of-Hadith-Jibril-About-Belief-Iman.html